meditations
from the soul
THE SOUL LANGUAGE OF GEMSTONES

Elizabeth Irvine

bright sky press
HOUSTON, TEXAS

2365 Rice Blvd., Suite 202
Houston, Texas 77005

Copyright © 2014 Elizabeth Irvine
No part of this book may be reproduced in any form or by any electronic or mechanical means, including information storage and retrieval devices or systems, without prior written permission from the publisher, except that brief passages may be quoted for reviews.

ISBN: 978-1-939055-97-2

10 9 8 7 6 5 4 3 2 1

Library of Congress Cataloging-in-Publication Data on file with publisher.

Editorial Direction, Lucy Herring Chambers
Photography, Elizabeth Irvine
Book Design, Wyn Bomar Design

PRINTED IN CANADA THROUGH FRIESENS

meditations
from the earth
THE SOUL LANGUAGE OF GEMSTONES

written and photographed by
Elizabeth Irvine

bright sky press
HOUSTON, TEXAS

As a child, one of my favorite things to do was to look for unique and beautiful rocks to collect. I felt a connection to them and stored them in a box under my bed, taking them out to hold and admire them. For my tenth birthday, my parents bought me a birthstone ring. The idea that this golden topaz resonated with the power of my birth made me feel the gem held special importance for me. Wearing my birthstone on my finger made me aware of my connection to my self and to the Earth in a new way. Ever since, I've been consciously aware of the energy a stone can give us —

        if we are open to noticing its power.

My work in helping women to find peace through healthy, whole living has led me to different paths, and it is exciting when they come together. For the last several years, I have been creating jewelry from semi-precious gemstones and using them in my personal life with affirmations relating to the unique qualities of their energy. Friends have asked me to share these crystal meditations, and this little book emerged from that request. Here, you will find the power of each gemstone's energy combined with the soulful clarity of an affirmation. My hope is that in taking the time to focus on the wisdom and beauty of the earth's jewels, you will see these qualities reflected in your own life, learn to SHINE BRIGHTLY from deep within your soul and tap into your pure potential.

As I worked to combine the beauty and effect of the gemstones in my jewelry, I came to understand more about their qualities and how it feels so comforting to have them near me as I navigate challenges in life. Through the meditation, an affirmation became clear and evolved very naturally. This practice allowed me to feel simultaneously more grounded and free, and with this clarity, choices in life were made more easily. In retrospect, it was as if the stones were teaching me to speak my own SOUL LANGUAGE.

Now, my intention is to pass this knowledge on to you — to help you become better acquainted with these gemstone meditations, to use them to dig deeper into your soul, to find the energy that is present in every aspect of your being and use it to grow and blossom.

A History Forged Deep Within | While a gem can be a crystal, a crystal cannot always be called a gem. A gemstone is a crystal that is considered more precious in value, usually due to its clarity and rareness. I love both crystals and gemstones for adornment but also, and perhaps more, for the beautiful emotion they create. For me, the richness of the feeling they bring to the world surpasses the value of their beauty. Taking the relationship with the stone beyond just owning it as an object, and connecting with a gemstone's energy is really about holding a DEEP RESEPECT for what the Earth has given us.

A crystal geode comes from the earth. It is a sparkling memory of what has always been. The crystal's lattice structure allows the geode to be carried through billions of years of evolution. This lattice pattern has a profound structural influence on the crystal, forming stones of great individuality.

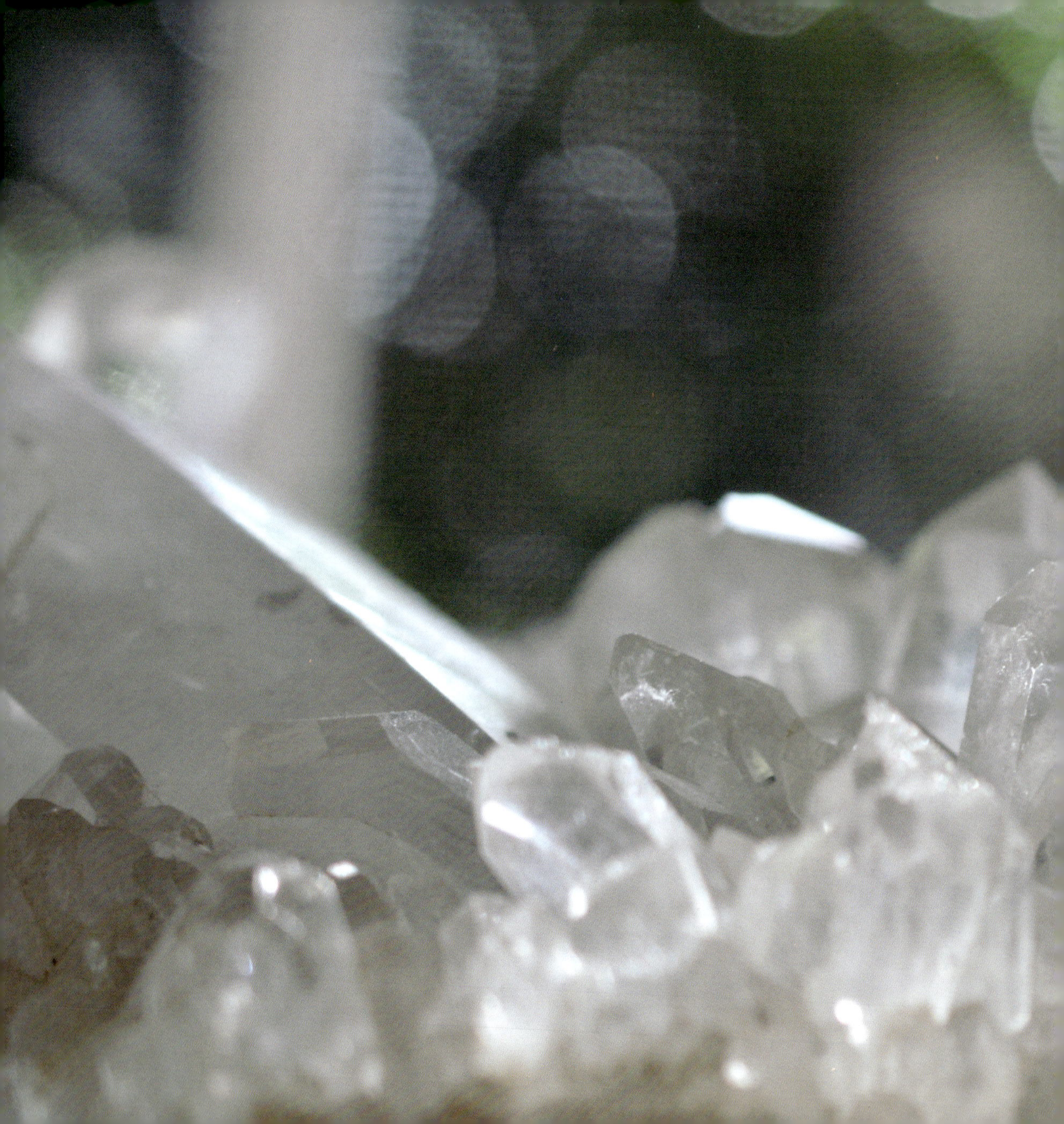

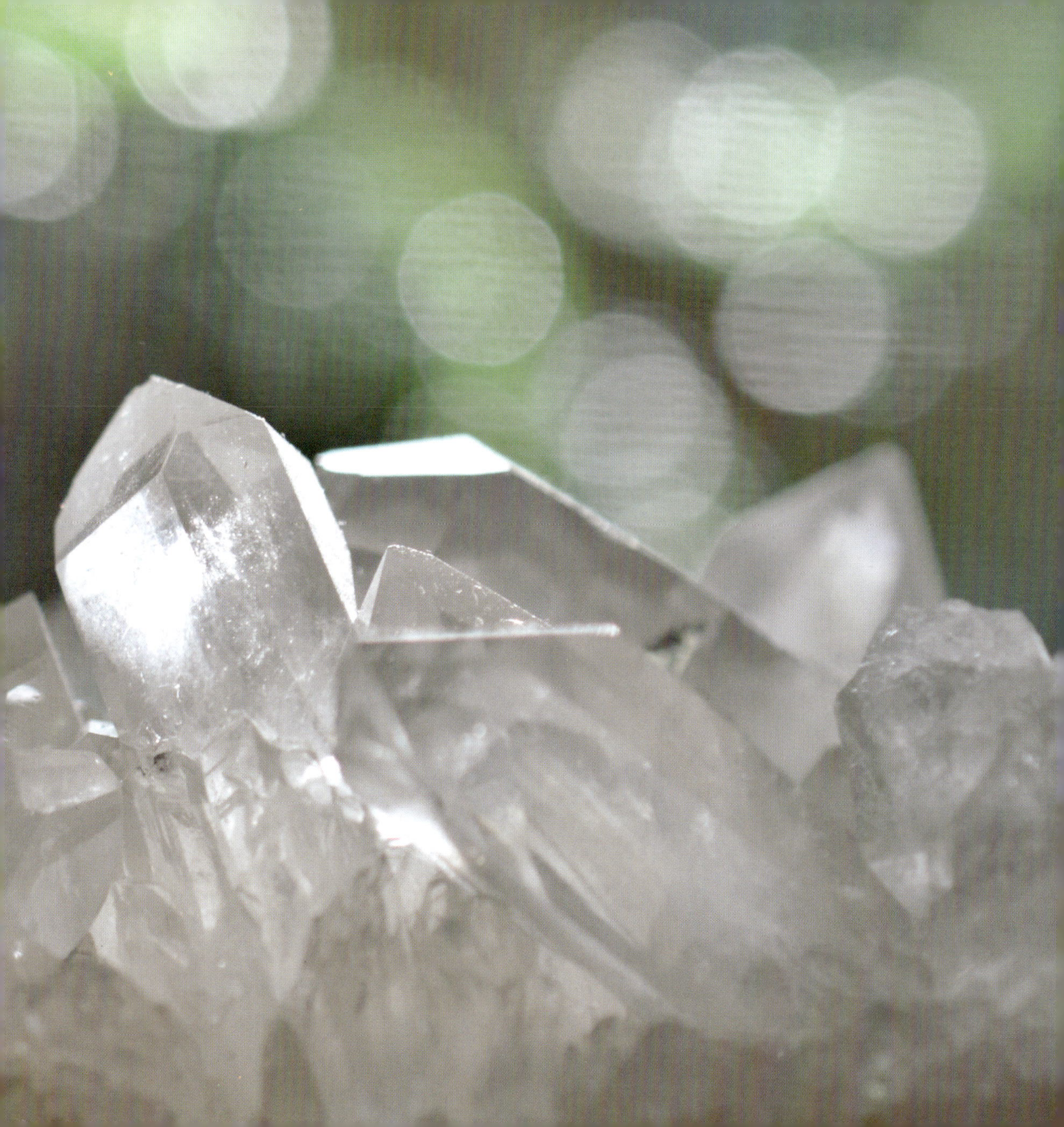

We only have to look at how different graphite and diamonds are in appearance, though each contains only carbon.

Not only beautiful, crystals act as resonators and transmitters — a silicon chip in a computer's memory, a quartz movement keeping time in a watch, an amplifier for a radio wave or a vehicle for creating a laser's precise incision. Quartz crystals have a charge that is said to be piezoelectric. The word *piezo* is Greek for "push." If a crystal can do all of that, perhaps it's reasonable to believe I could sense my birthstone sending me a feeling.

Appreciation for our Earth | If we look back into history, crystals and gemstones have held a revered place in our lives. They have been found in the tombs of ancient Egypt, adorning the breastplates of warriors, and sparkling in the crowns of sovereignty. The Bible references jewels, even explaining that the glory of God imparts "a radiance like a most rare jewel, like a jasper, clear as crystal." I believe that appreciating crystals keeps their energy active and draws them forward into modern times; if we don't appreciate them, their spirit is stifled, and the synergy drains. This need for our intention is

the same for all of the gifts we have in our lives. Gratitude and appreciation activate the response: Appreciate what we presently have in our life. Treat other human beings as we want to be treated. Take care of the Earth so that we have a balanced and nurturing home for generations to come.

How Do I Choose a Stone? | Let your intuition guide you, and you will find the stone's energetic qualities that will benefit you most. Each gemstone is a gift of the earth, vibrating to a certain frequency to help us feel qualities such as LOVE, BALANCE, CREATIVITY, ENERGY, or PEACE.

Recently, a friend from Santa Fe contacted me to ask what gemstone would help her most as she was starting a new job. I told her it was a personal process and advised she look at the gemstones and choose the one that called to her. The next day, she told me she was totally in love with blue lace agate. As this stone's energy is about expressing your voice through clear communication, I suggested this *affirmation* to her: I communicate through my words, and so my words become my reality. My friend said, "Well that seems appropriate. My new job is to be editor of a magazine! " She learned how to

TRUST HER OWN INSTINCTS and chose the stone that would be helpful to her and would align her with her highest potential.

To illustrate how the meditations flow from each stone's energy, here is another example. The stone chrysoprase holds properties of grace and balance. A potential affirmation aligning with this gemstone might be I feel whole and balanced as I see nature, and others around me in their natural state of grace. When we add an affirmation inspired through the gemstone's energy, we begin to align with powerful magnetics. We learn how to open a doorway to self-awareness that brings forth our instinctive natural beauty, and we effortlessly shine.

Affirm What You Know is True | To truly know your self is possibly the greatest gift of a lifetime. Affirmations help guide us on that path. They create clarity, form intention, and lead us to our true essence. They allow us to guide our choices from deep within. At the core, each of us is perfect and and whole, a DIVINE LIGHT.

It was about twenty years ago when I first came to know about the power of meditation and affirmations. As I lay flat on my back in the "pose of a corpse," my eyes lightly closed, a soft blanket covering me with my breath soft and full, time stood still. I heard the voice of my swami yoga teacher, "In the practice of yoga nidra we deeply relax, form the seed of our sankalpa (a short positive statement for change), and plant this affirmation in fertile ground to take deep roots and grow." In this quiet STILL SPACE, I felt a deep and healing peace, and became re-acquainted with my true nature.

How Do I Choose an Affirmation? | The five-thousand-year-old Sanskrit word *sankalpa* translates as *san* "union" and *kalpa* "possibility"— the possibility exists within. When stated with positive language in an aware state of mind, the affirmation will eventually manifest. I use the word affirmation interchangeably with *sankalpa*; a vow, a commitment to myself and a request to guide my choices.

How do you begin to find your affirmation? The process begins with becoming quiet and still, so that you may hear — from deep within — so you can listen

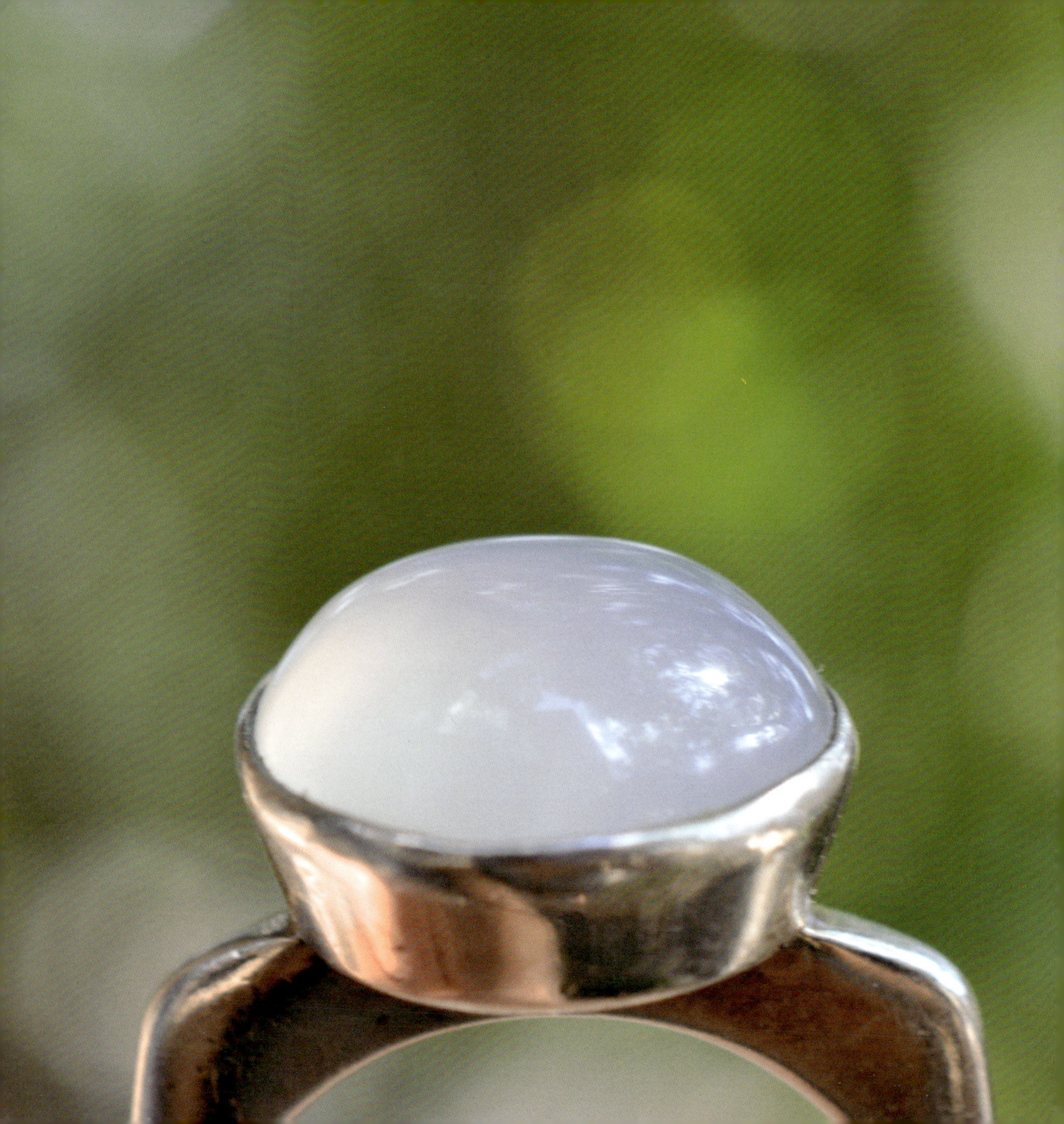

to what your heart knows to be true. The idea is already there, just waiting TO BE HEARD. Then state your feeling, with a deep awareness of truth, staying in the present tense. For example, instead of, "I want to become more healthy," the affirmation becomes, "My body is vibrantly healthy." It is not "I will not eat junk food;" it is "My body is a temple that I only nourish with the highest-quality food."

The Jewelry Project | When I completed my yoga education, as a graduation gift, my swami gave me a simple sandalwood prayer mala. I loved wearing this mala, and my yoga students asked where they could get one, too. This is how the idea came to me to develop a prayer-style mala adding gemstones to the design, which I now call Serenity Beads. I like to think of each of them as a *talisman,* something to bring comfort and act as a reminder to connect to my higher self throughout the day. My yoga nidra education and learning to form a *sankalpa* led me to combine this self-awareness language with gemstones. The idea was born to create jewelry around the energy of a gemstone and use it to cultivate deeper meaning in life. In retrospect, it seems inevitable that I would begin pairing the pieces with affirmations.

Uncover the Goodness Within | The essence of gemstone and affirmation practice is learning how to get in touch with what you really want for your life. A bigger house, a new car, or an exotic vacation can be lovely supplements, but they have very little to do with core values such as health, happiness, integrity, or a sense of purpose.

An affirmation is an evolution that BEGINS TODAY. In order to figure out where we want to go in the future, we must first focus our energy on where we are now and begin to look at our bigger life picture. With practice, we begin to soften and INVITE IN MORE PATIENCE, learn to acknowledge what is important, feel true power, and shift the paradigm of values. We create the experience of my friend in Santa Fe who used her own ability to choose the right stone and align her affirmation with her individual needs. In learning to affirm what we want, we feed our subconscious a positive light-filled beacon to lead us home.

Begin Speaking Soul Language | Right now, imagine the quiet still space that exists deep within you. Take a few long, deep, soothing breaths—in… and out. INHALE. EXHALE. Notice how your breath begins to MAKE SPACE IN YOUR BODY and also creates more space between your thoughts. Use your breath to let go of built-up stress, and re-connect—even just briefly—to the deepest part of you that is whole and pure. Your true nature remains unchanged whether you remember to honor it or not. Bring your awareness to deep within, to your own divine light. Now ask the question, "What would I like to change in my life?" You are sending a message from your conscious mind to your subconscious. It is not a wish or a hope, it's an intention for positive change. Allow this message to come into your awareness. Form this thought into a short positive statement for change. Repeat your resolve to yourself. Be patient with the process. Inspiration and ideas will always surface as you learn to become quieter and listen.

Namaste is an increasingly popular Sanskrit word that translates, "I bow to the divinity, the light deep within your soul; and you bow to the divinity, the light deep within my soul." One word, *namaste*, means all of that. Transport yourself to this feeling of humble adoration. Hold reverence for the message of the gemstone you choose to help you, state your positive resolve —

and start speaking soul language.

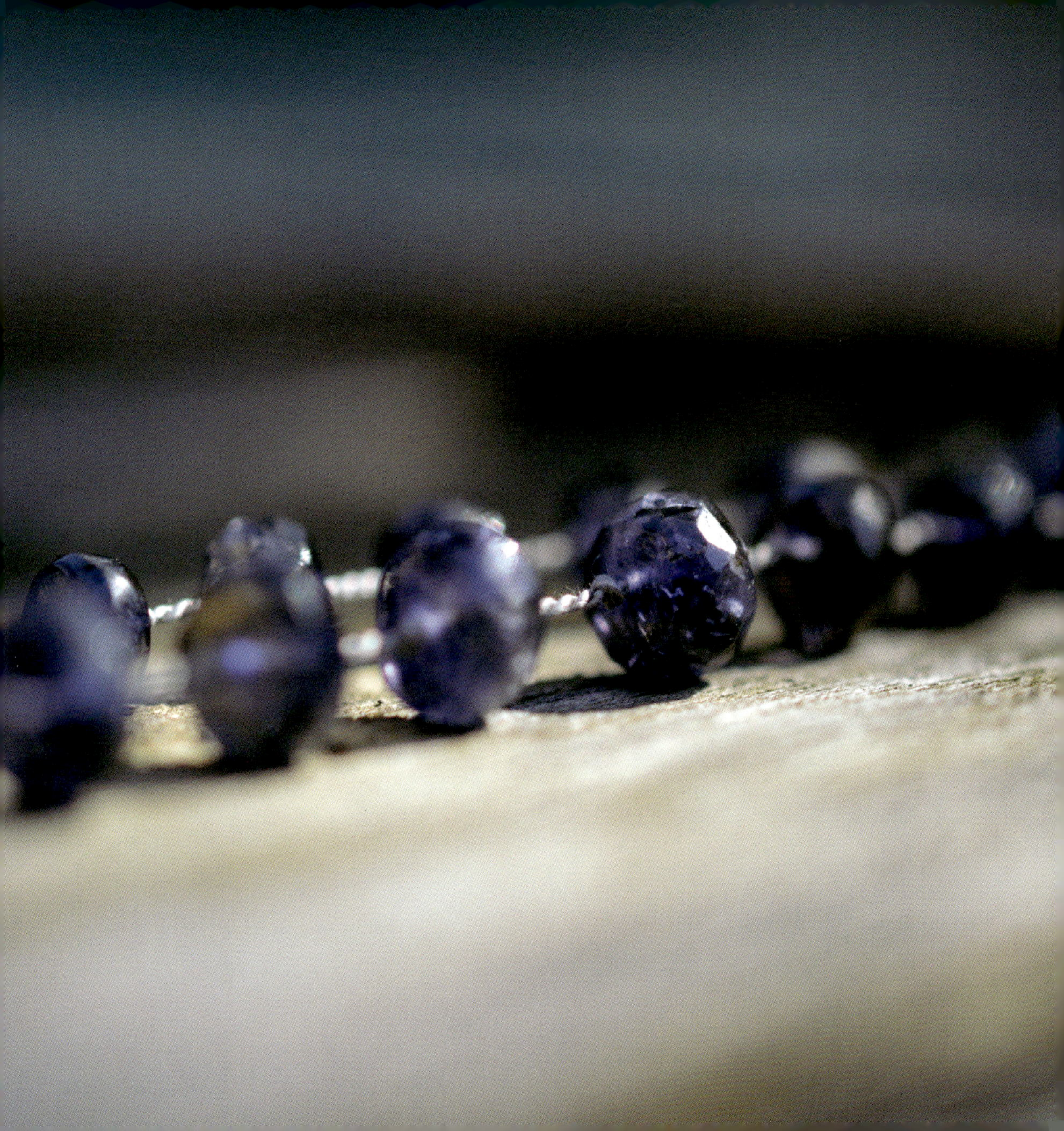

Amazonite

harmony | truth | communication

Truth shines from deep within our souls. Amazonite helps us communicate our own truth to reflect a higher, more aligned vibration. As we communicate deep truths we teach others through our harmonious example.

What I teach teaches me.

Amber

light | fossilized tree resin | ancient wisdom

Mother Earth holds balanced ancient wisdom, giving and receiving in harmony with the seasons throughout time. The synthesis of light by plants and trees creates Amber. As our consciousness connects to universal perfection, the body heals itself.

I call forth light.
I find the innate
healing within me,
and I feel energized.

Amethyst

higher self | ethereal | spiritual growth

To admire something naturally beautiful transports us to a better place. The vibrant beauty of Amethyst connects us to an ethereal part of our nature, our higher self.

I connect to my higher self and feel my inner beauty radiating outward.

Aquamarine

calm | clear communication | water

Not all power comes from force. Through Aquamarine we feel the cool and soothing natural power of water, and we allow ourselves to flow with the current.

My voice is calm and I communicate with clarity.

Blue Lace Agate

grace | communication | free expression

Our words create our reality. When mind, heart and spirit are in union we become both strong and sensitive. Through the graceful power of Blue Lace Agate, spiritual truths can be expressed to instill the positive within the hearts of humanity. We communicate with clarity.

I communicate through my words, and my words become my reality.

Carnelian

creative | sensual | freedom

The "dwelling place of the self" is our true essence. Carnelian's fiery orange color leads us to the life force within and taps into our sensuality and creativity.

I honor the dwelling place within — my sensuality and creativity. I feel free.

Celestite

angelic | clear communication | guidance

Angel means messenger. According to the Bible, angels are purely spiritual creations who act as liaisons between Heaven and Earth to guard us and bring us messages. Celestite reminds us to pay attention to the feelings and messages of angelic guidance.

I honor my intuition and the unlimited divine resource of angelic communication.

Chalcedony

soothe | balance | brotherhood for all

To feel peace is to let go of day-to-day stress and replace these feelings with a sense of calm. In this place, Chalcedony allows us to feel our humanness and creates a soothing balance between us and the world.

In this place of peaceful balance, I feel a connection to everything and everyone.

Chrysoprase

balance yin and yang | grace | apple-green natural energy

Yin and Yang are complementary opposites within a greater whole. Chrysoprase helps bring balance, and therefore we feel heartfelt compassion as our natural state of grace. As we open eyes of compassion, we bring a natural effortless balance to body and mind.

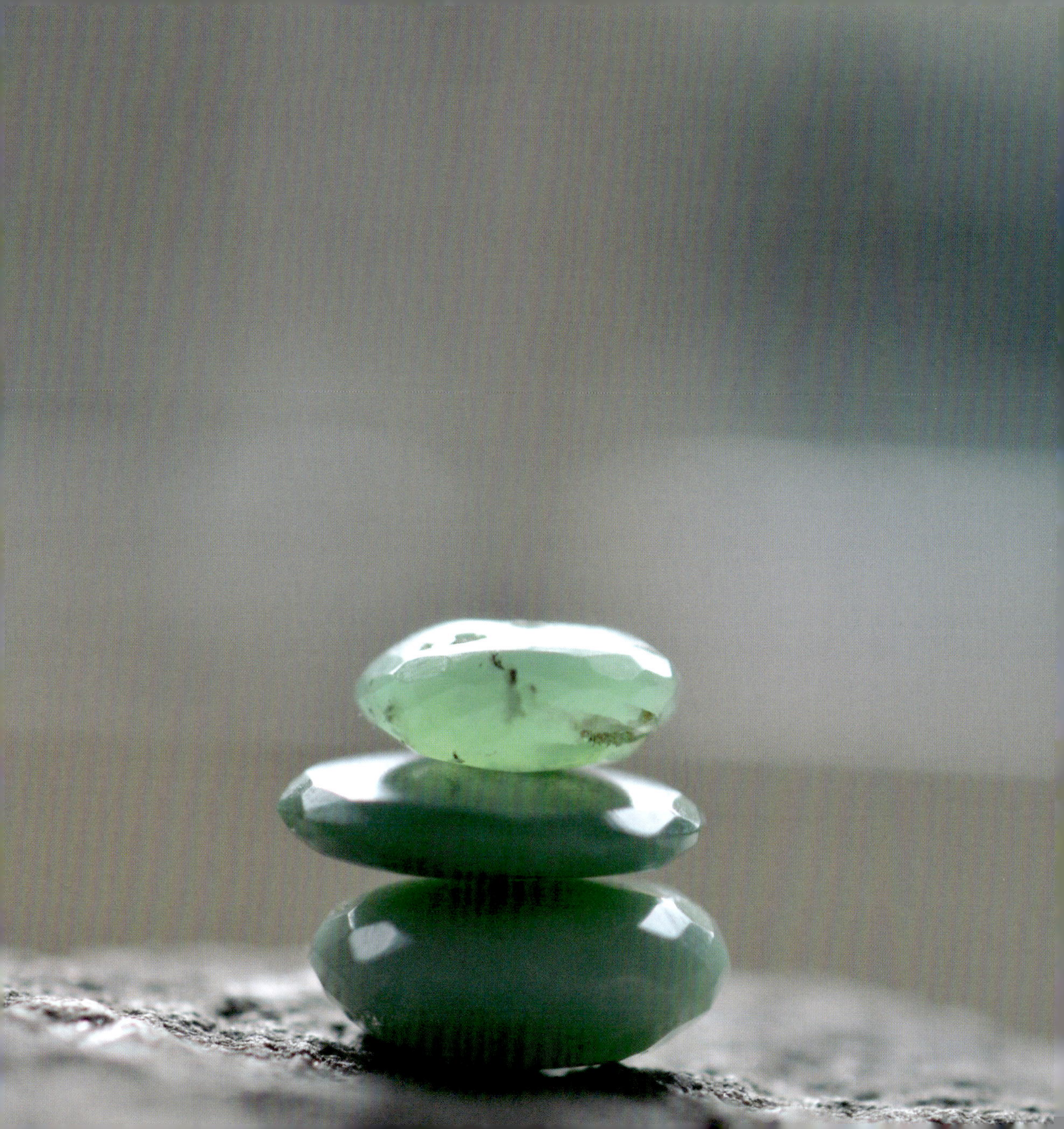

I see myself as part of unified creation and view others around me in their natural state of beauty and grace. I feel whole.

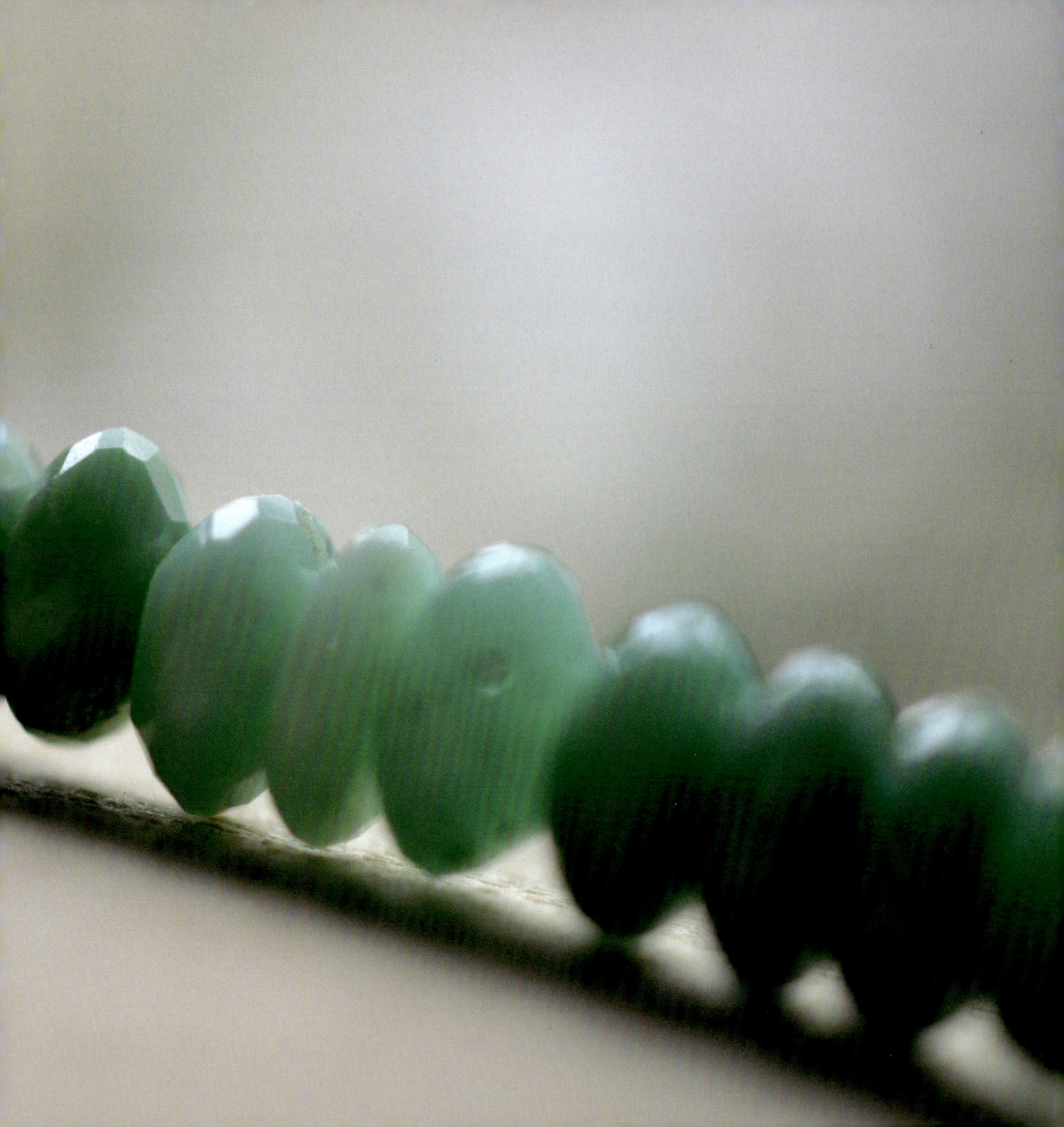

Citrine

balance | clearing | mental clarity

The word Citrine comes from the French *citron,* lemon. The yellow color of the sun's energy resonates with our life force. When we feel energized and clear, we radiate clarity from within.

I am a bright light
radiating from the inside out.

Danburite

grace | love | angelic communication

Angelic messages often come as a subtle nudge through an emotion or physical feeling. When we allow our heart to be open, we become more sensitive to the angelic realms. The translucent pink color of Danburite creates a feeling full of light and grace. It connects us to our heart's desires and the love and well-being of others.

As I expand my awareness into love, light, and grace, I call forth my angels to guide me.

Garnet

grounding | secure | body awareness

The commitment to remain focused on simple basic care for our bodies can feel natural and easy. The grounded secure feeling Garnet brings reminds us to hold awareness for the body and to "feel good in our own skin."

I feel solid and sure of myself.
I attract positive vibrations that
come from this secure feeling.

Howlite

calm communication | awareness | grounding

The combination of reasoning, observation, and patience is a powerful life skill. Through the grounded feeling Howlite brings, we are patient and calm in our communication. In this place we become the observer of our thoughts and actions, and we practice the art of responding, rather than reacting.

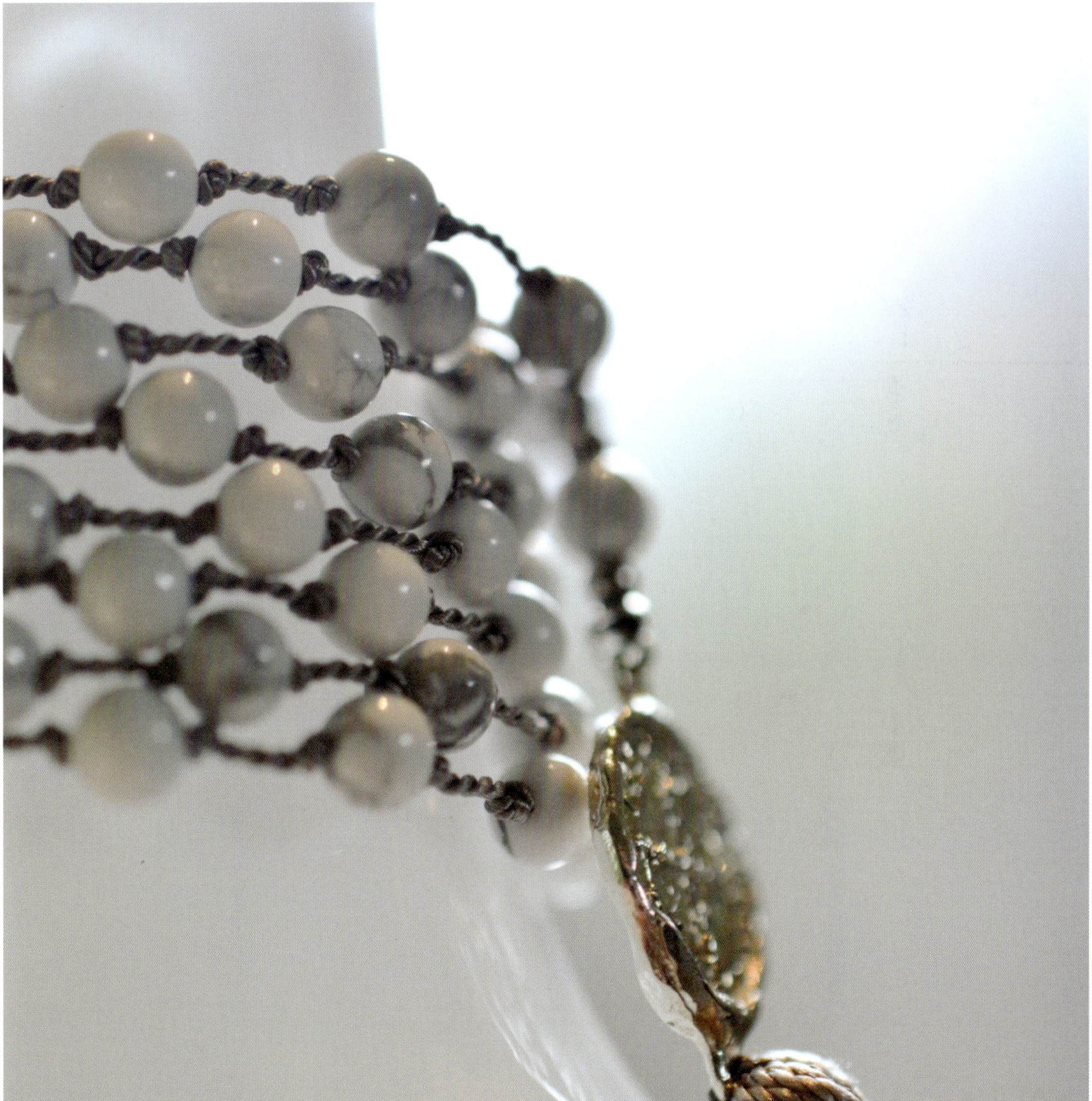

I step back and become the observer. I communicate with the patient awareness that comes from inner calm.

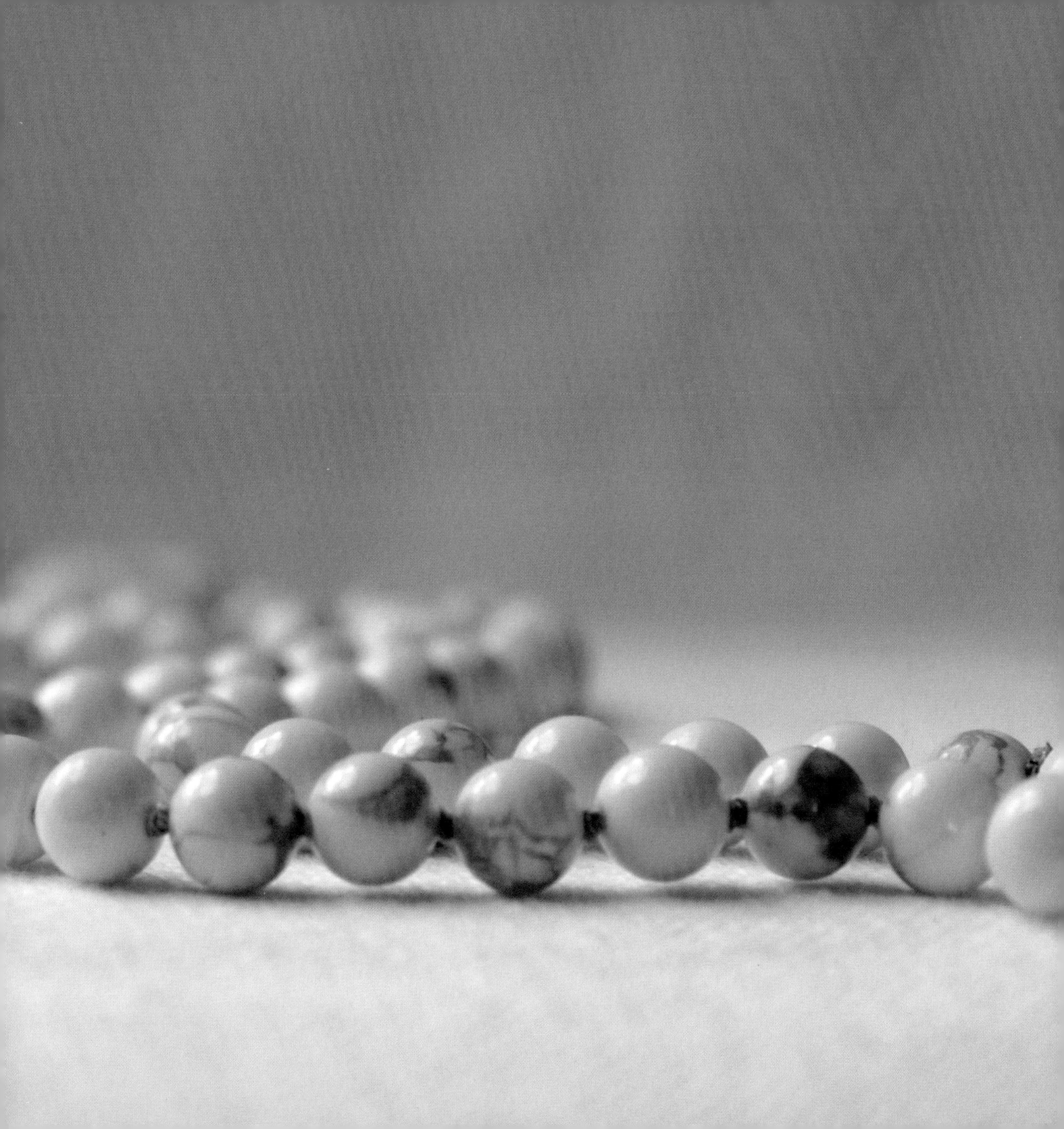

Iolite

inner vision | intuition | confidence

When we learn to read between the lines, we experience a sense of strong confidence in who we are and the choices we make. Iolite's indigo tone harmonizes with our inner vision. We honor our sixth sense and trust our intuition.

I allow myself the time to notice what I am feeling. I trust what I sense, and I am confident and at peace with my choices.

Jade

dream | nature | abundance

Dreams are part of our heart and go to the depths of our soul to fulfill our destiny. Whether it's remembering our dreams or building them, we must follow where they lead. Jade's green color represents the life force of nature, always an abundant reminder that there is always enough available.

I pay attention to my dreams, and I align the feelings they bring forth with the choices in my day.

Kyanite

meditation | never needs clearing | amplifier of high frequency energy

Meditation brings us feelings of peace, energy, clarity — gifts we give ourselves. Time spent in silence becomes sacred space. Simply dedicating a time to close our eyes and focus on our breath builds a haven for us. Holding Kyanite while in meditation creates a clear path.

I focus on the
soothing rhythm
of my breath.
I feel at peace.

Labradorite

magic | synchronicity | higher awareness

Life brings signposts. When we choose to notice and acknowledge these serendipitous occurrences, they become a navigation system and help keep life on course. When synchronicity appears, it confirms that we are connecting with the magic of our inner wisdom. If we stay awake and pay attention, our destiny unfolds as a series of signposts.

I recognize the synchronicity in my life.
I pay attention to the messages I receive.

Lapis Lazuli

inner vision | divine inspiration | balance

The antidote to the increasing speed of modern life is to find a quiet still space everyday. During meditation self-knowledge and understanding come to light through our inner vision. Lapis enhances a connection to divine inspiration and is a beautiful stone to use in meditation.

In my balanced state, I claim the power of my inner vision.

Larimar

healing | soothing | communication

Worry and doubt create tension in our bodies and steal our energy. Larimar helps connect to the healing capacity within each of us. In this quiet still space, we experience healing and soothing feelings and communicate them to the specific needs of our bodies.

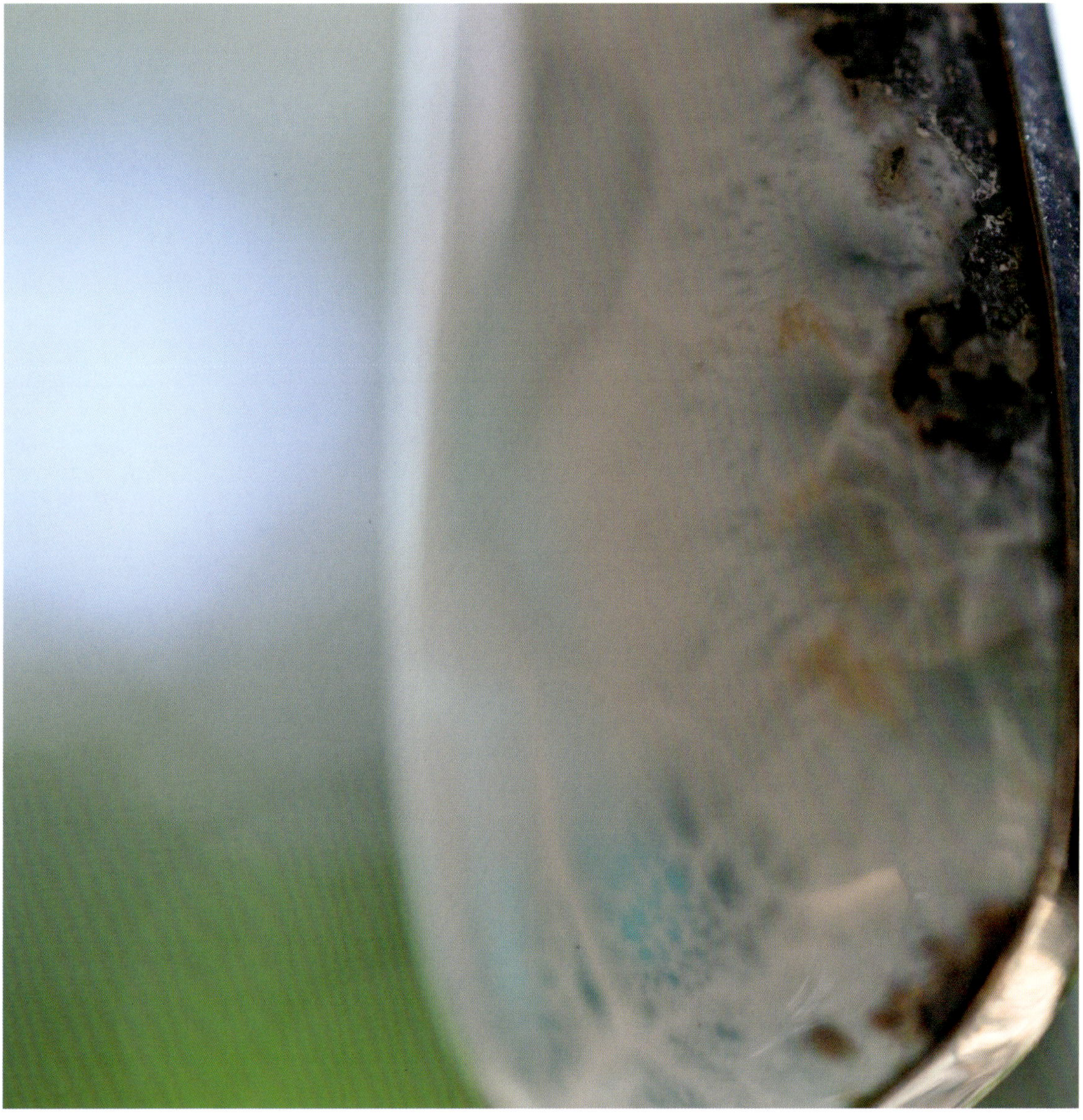

As I allow myself to heal,
I heal others who are near me.

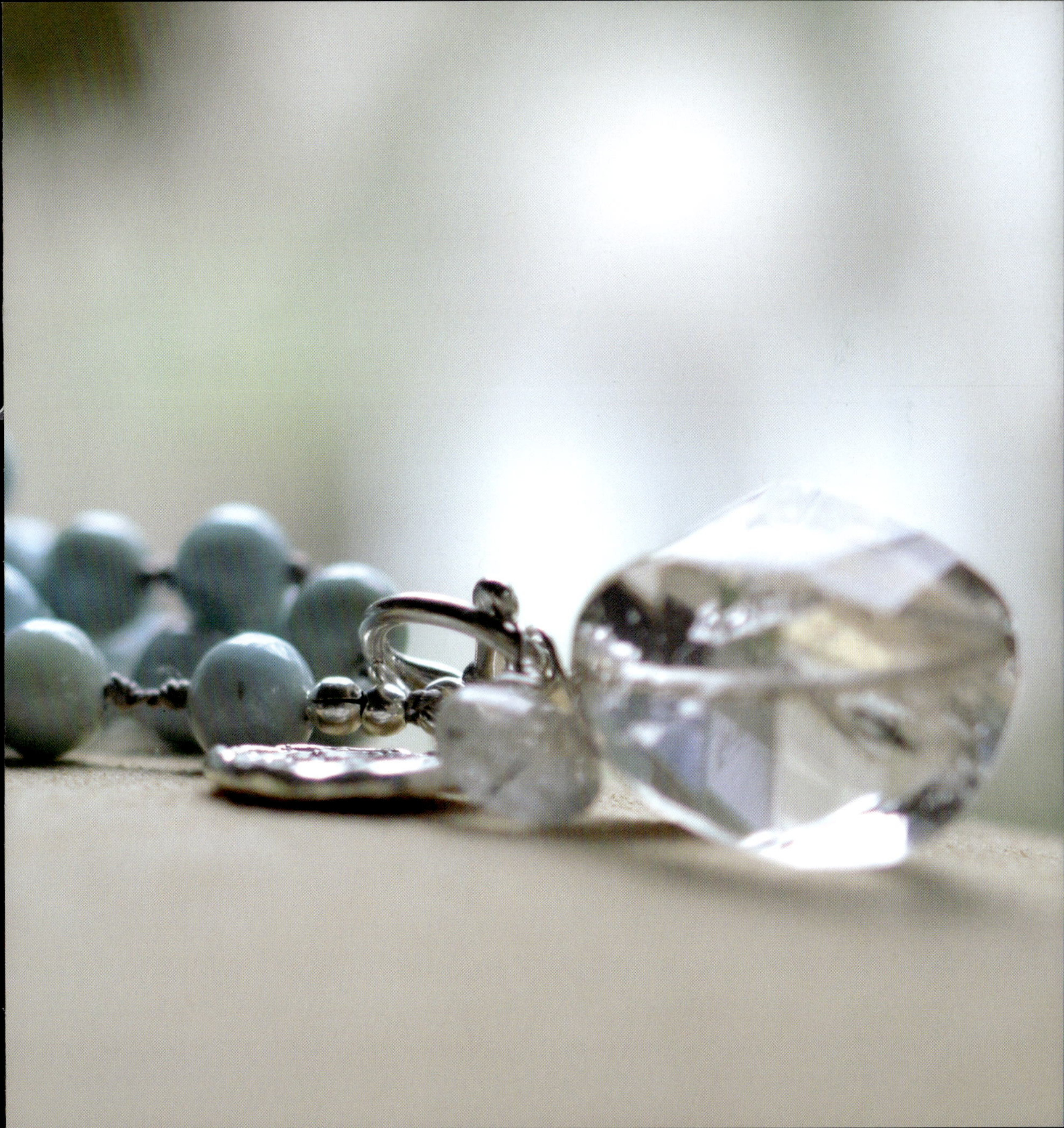

Moonstone

lunar | feminine power | intuition

Ocean tides, yearly calendars, women's cycles, farmers crops, all are influenced by lunar cycles. Wearing Moonstone during the new and full moon brings us back to our inner goddess wisdom.

I connect
to my natural
feminine power
and own my
intuitive
wisdom.

Peridot

warm & friendly | positive power | strength

The sun's warm and friendly energy heals body and soul. The positive energy of Peridot is like a link between Heaven and Earth. Floating through the rays of sunshine, a gift from nature's soul energy shines before us.

The sun's warm energy brings me strength and positive power throughout my day.

Peruvian Opal

nature | precious | healing

Known in Latin as *opalus,* in Sanskirt as *upala,* opal means "precious stone." The colors of nature shine through in Peruvian Opal. The combinations of water, greenery, and the Earth create a sense of balance and healing within our own nature.

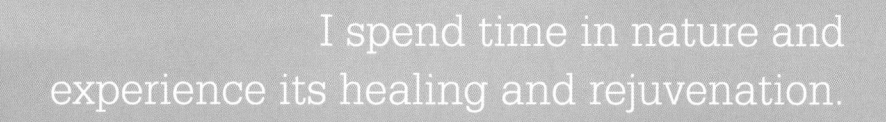

I spend time in nature and experience its healing and rejuvenation.

Pink Calcite

well-being | support | comfort

Well-being comes from healthy balance, nothing in excess. Pink Calcite feels comforting and soothing. During time of dis-ease, I remember my state of balanced perfection and return to a loving space. In this place I know all is well.

Everything in moderation creates a healthy balance.

Picture Jasper

nurturer | connected to earth | protection

The abundance of beauty in nature is also a reflection of our own true nature. The patterns of Picture Jasper, the scenes within the stone, hold deep messages from nature. Gazing at them connects us to the Earth, a beautiful way to re-align our energy, regain strength and security.

The harmony of nature is a reflection of my own true nature.

Rhodochrosite

heart | comfort | childlike innocence

Being light of heart is a powerful healer. We learn to tap into our true essence through this happy feeling. Wearing Rhodochrosite soothes the heart and brings comfort to the soul. We feel a sweet child-like innocence, let go of our cares, and smile.

In child-like innocence,
I feel connected to my heart and soul.

Onyx

strength | focus | discipline

There is a wonderful sense of satisfaction when we complete a task. Black Onyx helps us stay grounded and strong. In this place we are disciplined and focused.

As I work, I have the clarity and discipline to reach today's goal.

Pink Tourmaline

loving consciousness | heart | sacred space

Truly, one of the finest things in life is to know who we are. As we honor our sacred space, we connect with the synthesis of love and spirituality. Pink Tourmaline helps us surrender to love, and our hearts feel whole and healed. We trust in the power of love.

I am a beacon of light, living in love and leaving lower vibrations behind.

Clear Quartz

energy | magnifier | "piezo"

Quartz crystal has what is known as piezoelectricity. It transforms electromagnetic energy into mechanical energy, such as movement in a watch. This versatile crystal can amplify any energy, including thoughts and intentions.

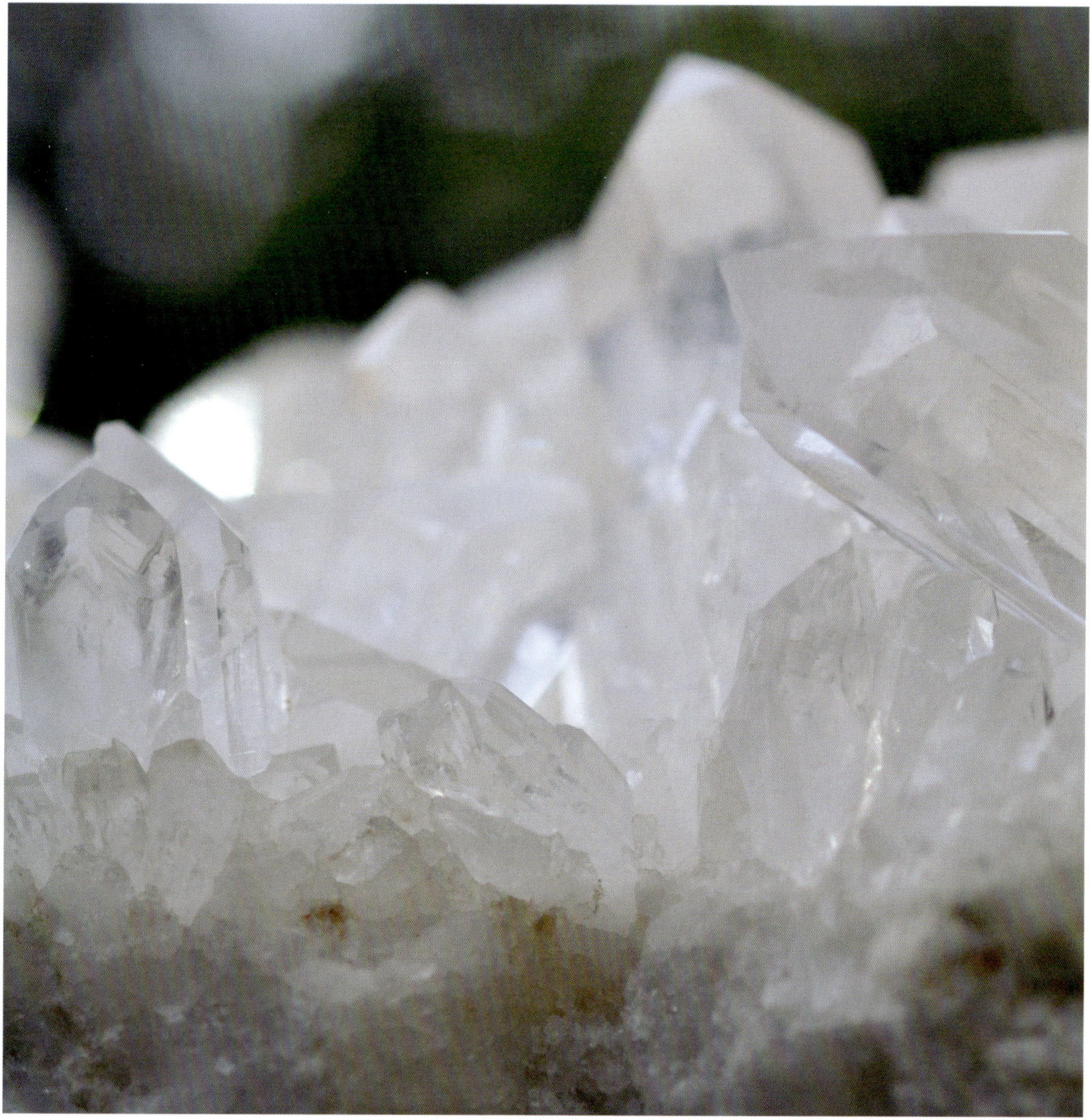

God made me an angel of energy, and
I feel this energy magnified within me.

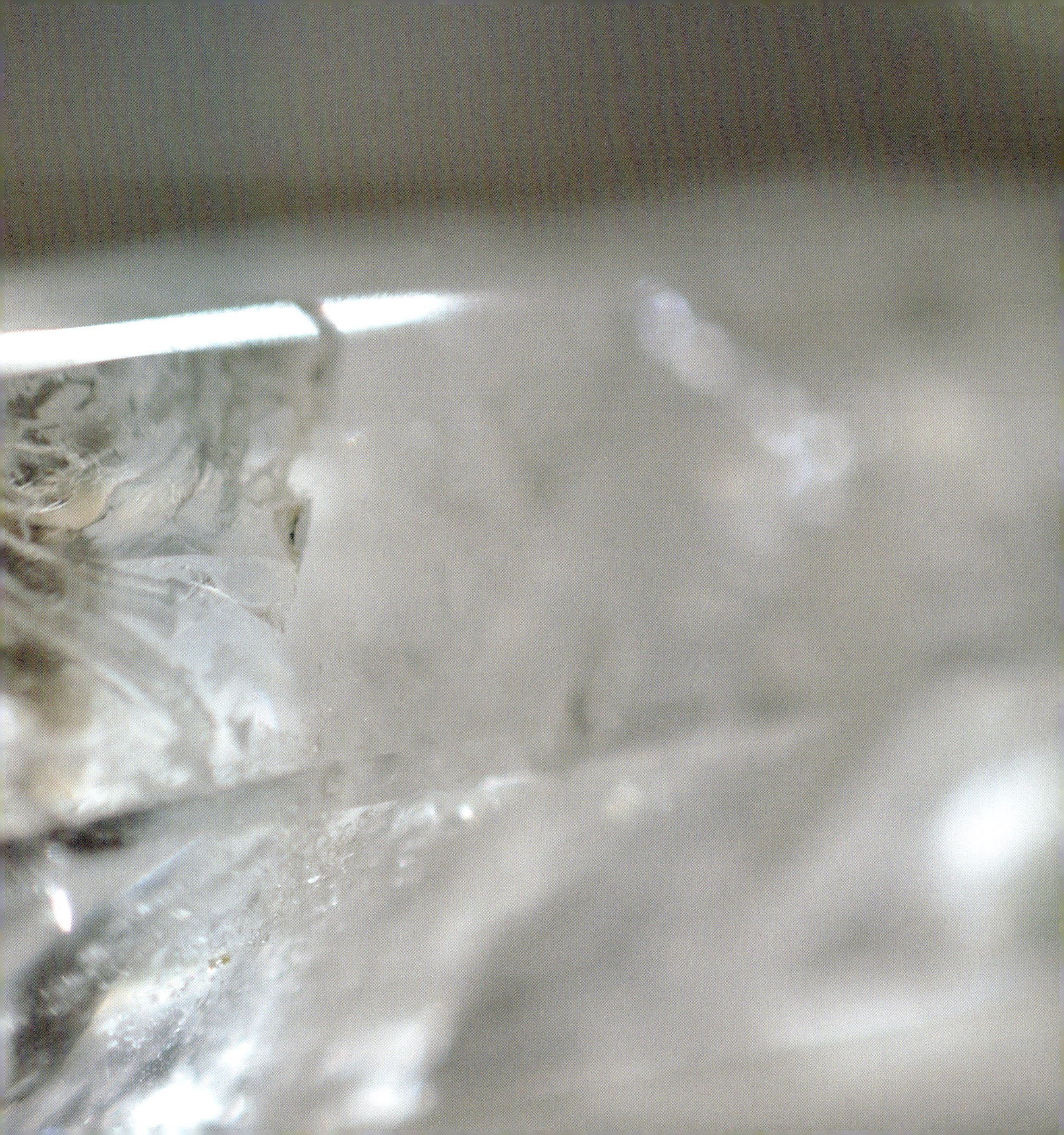

Rose Quartz

love | self-love | love for others

Love is all there is. When our hearts are open, love is all around. Rose Quartz creates a tender feeling, full of compassion. Whether it's healing self-love or love for others, love is a powerful remedy.

I see myself filled with love and radiate its warmth to everyone and everything.

Rutilated Quartz

magnified quartz | higher plane | divine inspiration

The plant kingdom's life force is like a spirit body around nature's creation. Rutilated Quartz, an amplified quartz crystal, allows us to tap into the life force around us. In this ethereal place we feel in harmony with our divine purpose.

I feel connected to higher energy, and my positive thoughts are magnified.

Smokey Quartz

grounding | clearing | organized

When we allow our feet to sink into the ground, we feel plugged into the Earth's energy. Smokey Quartz brings forth the feeling of being connected to the Earth. Through this feeling of unobstructed connection, our head clears. Clear space heals us on many levels. From this simple, centered place we feel solid and protected.

With my feet solidly on the ground, I feel centered and whole. Clarity comes freely.

Selenite

air purifier | meditation | clarity

Sacred space nurtures our soul. When we are in a place that feels good we find it easier to think, dream, and connect with the best part of who we are. Selenite is a natural purifier for our space. Regular clearing of our space is essential to keep clarity of mind and expand our awareness.

I commit to create daily sacred space. In this place I find clarity and expanded awareness.

Turquoise

heals | protective | Mother Earth

The image of sky and water in a stone is a protective gift from Mother Earth. Healing comes through our acceptance of our wholeness, what we have learned on our life's journey, mistakes and all. Turquoise is a true healer of the spirit. As we connect to this healing, protective stone, we feel blessed with a grateful heart.

I own my wholeness and speak with truth.

Peace
Clarity
Calm
Love
Gratitude
Joy

The Earth speaks soul language.
Are you listening?

To some of my best soul teachers,

Allie, Sarah & Sam

May your generation's language
be the change that raises the vibration
to create a better earth for us all.